The Cosmic Oval

The Cosmic Oval
an essay with sleep songs

ELLA FINER

Commissioned by the Jencks Foundation at The Cosmic House

Published in 2025 by Spiral House, an imprint of Silver Press.

ISBN-13: 978-1-0682409-0-4

Design by Rose Nordin
Typeset in Adobe Caslon Pro by Alice Spawls
Printed and bound in the UK by CPI

EU GPSR Authorised Representative: Logos Europe,
9 rue Nicolas Poussin, 17000, La Rochelle, France.
contact@logoseurope.eu

1 3 5 7 9 10 8 6 4 2

THE COSMIC HOUSE

CONTENTS

In a sense, every life that is recounted is offered as an example; we write in order to attack or defend a view of the universe, and to set forth a system of conduct which is our own.

Marguerite Yourcenar, translated by Grace Frick,
Memoirs of Hadrian

To write by shreds, by storm clouds, by visions, by violent chapters, in the present as in the archpast, in pre-vision, in the true chaos of verbal tenses, crossing over years and oceans at a god's pace, with the past on my right and the future on my left – this is forbidden in academies, it is permitted in apocalypses.

Hélène Cixous, translated by Eric Prenowitz,
Stigmata

Poetry is not only dream and vision; it is the skeleton architecture of our lives. It lays the foundations for a future of change, a bridge across our fears of what has never been before.

Audre Lorde,
Your Silence Will Not Protect You: Essays and Poems

Preface

Stories of spacetime move in many ways. Across millennia, humans have given shape to the beginnings of the universe through myriad explanatory models and imaginative systems, each with their own persuasive dimensions, their own calls to attend to the production of knowledge and cultural expression in relation to the immensity of the cosmos. The human urge is towards the microcosm: a distillation of vast, unknowable systems into forms that can be seen, touched, lived with and within.

The Cosmic House in West London, designed by writer and architect Charles Jencks and writer, artist and garden designer Maggie Keswick Jencks in the early 1980s, is one such form: a physical manifestation of Jencks's pluralist vision of the cosmos and the human within it. The House is full of mirrors, with rooms designed for each of the seasons; to enter it is to step into an architectural kaleidoscope of time, a model containing models, every part offering its own cosmological-cultural system.

The Cosmic Oval, the elliptical entrance hall of The Cosmic House, is one of the constituent models. It is animated by a wraparound Cultural History Frieze designed by Jencks in collaboration with Keswick Jencks, and painted by William Stok in 1984. The Frieze offers a speculative star map of twelve painted figures, a constellated diagram of several great waves in our developing understandings of the cosmos through religious, scientific and cultural shifts. 'Designed to be pretentious – to pretend to more knowledge and wisdom than we can possibly have', the Cosmic Oval is a model in which the conditions of 'knowing' are performed.[1] What makes the twelve cultural figures glow with symbolic potential also renders them icons of impossibility: they bring the worth of their historical measure, as well as the limits of what they are called upon to represent.

In the Frieze, the twelve figures gather just below the height of the ceiling, among galactic swirls moving from Big Bang to black hole – poised variously in deep conversation and ponderous reflection, their glances by turn conspiratorial and curious. If you and I were together in this mirrored room of seventeen doors – elliptical dome and diagram above and beneath us – such swift description would likely go unspoken. I might raise my hand to the left of the door, as others have done for me, introducing Thomas Jefferson and Hannah Arendt, giving names to the faces. I might continue clockwise through Imhotep, Pythagoras, Tao Yuanming, Hadrian, Abbot Suger, Erasmus, Alessandro de Angelis, John Donne, Borromini and Prince Ito. I might gesture to some of the charms: the astrolabe held by de Angelis, the broken column and the talismanic miniature of St Ivo's spire. But as for what to make of this gathered twelve and their symbols, as for speculating on a potential conversation between the philosophers, architects, cultural and historical figures in the Frieze, this I would leave to your own sensibilities, your own work of interpretation and explanation formed and forming in what you choose to hear, attune to and pick up, in the cacophonous energies of the dome.

Listening reveals the blurred edges of historical representation – not only in how each of us hears and defines the subject anew but also in the ways influence, presence and tradition circulate beyond simple chronologies. What is at stake in models of existence which make space for certain bodies and their stories of the world? What kinds of knowledge or experience fall out of a created symbolic order? With what singular or collective impulses are such models made? With what networks of collaboration, conscious or otherwise?

Knowledge emerges as much through what is obscure, peripheral and incomplete as through what is granted the light and legibility of recognition – what *appears*. And so I turn to the night – as I often do – for what it opens and offers to modes of knowing that are intuitive, nonlinear, quantum. And in the night, sleep – or something closer to sleep than wakefulness: a state described by poet Anne Carson as 'a glimpse of something incognito'.[2] The Sleep Song – an invented lyric form I have composed through listening to the shards of what humans leave to time – holds to the value of *something incognito*. Seven songs for the Cosmic Oval unfold in what follows, with glimpses of the ear as well as the eye, when 'what is incognito hides from us because it has something worth hiding'.[3]

PEOPLE AT DINNER, OR SLEEPING

There is a subtle magic in entering a scene from the sleep side, Anne Carson's brilliant description of the effect she experiences inside a childhood dream of her 'green living room', which makes strange the intimately familiar:

> It was the same old living room as ever, I knew it well, nothing was out of place. And yet it was utterly, certainly, different. Inside its usual appearance the living room was as changed as if it had gone mad . . . as far as I can recall, I explained the dream to myself by saying that I had caught the living room sleeping. I had entered it from the sleep side.[4]

I have yet to dream of The Cosmic House; my experience of this house has always been a wakeful encounter from the sleep side. In the room where I have been writing, wardrobes smile at me like owls, the carpet swirls to mimic green malachite, and there are two handles on every door. The light is bright and warm and it's not that I never feel awake, but I always feel I'm dreaming. This room, at the top of the house, has a bed – an unspoken invitation to sleep, or at least to imagine it – to hold open the door to sleep, to 'the border-land between living and not living'.[5]

Written on the back of one of several copies of Charles Jencks's 'Program for the Entrance Ellipse' is a stream of numbered handwritten notes, among which is a biro-penned fragment considering the depiction of the twelve historical figures of the Frieze.[6] Extending a line of thought about a major preoccupation of the Oval – the relationship of cosmic time and cultural time – Jencks notes a possible manifestation for the cosmic symposium, as 'people at dinner. Or sleeping'.

This note has stayed with me like a stage direction, or part of a blueprint to be activated in the future. Full of instructions, programs, lists, diagrams and sketches, the Archive is an expanded score: abundant and in continual motion across a span of forty years.

Yes, you can enter the Cosmic Oval as a finished 'room'; you can walk through it into the Winter and Spring rooms, gazing up as you go at the Frieze of ancient-to-modern luminaries as selected and consigned to egg tempera in the summer of 1984. Yet, this is not a settled monument or ode to cultural and cosmic revolutions. It is vibrantly *unsettled.*

This is a group of figures at dinner, or sleeping (and this ambivalent state of 'being/not being' I take to be integral), with the 'cosmic dance' swirling about them, 'all these moving shapes and spirals'.[7] They are simultaneously *in, against and part of* the universe on the move – the universe which, as the physicist Brian Greene writes, 'we have come to know is transitory. From planets to stars, solar systems to galaxies, black holes to swirling nebulae, nothing is everlasting.'[8]

SLEEP SONG

. . . if everything is moving, here is not here. Even when there is a here, it is not exactly here, but still an elsewhere . . . I am here, in the night, a night composed of *nows and thens and some-days*. And you, fellow traveller, are with me, your speech still shifting the dark air. *Everything is moving.*

We are standing outside the door to the house, listening to hushed conversation coming from inside, catching sentences – *little drifter* – fugitive across vocal registers *. . . distant galaxies are on the move. They're all rushing away . . .*

A question from inside – *why are we here?* – dissolves into deep breathing: many bodies' inhaling-exhaling like waves breaking in and out of time. *Anticipating the future is as unavoidable and commonplace as breathing.*

This soft breath of twelve *people at dinner, or sleeping. They are both* I whisper and you mouth *magic* without making a sound.

//

If everything is moving
here is not here
   not exactly here
still an elsewhere

I am here
      in the night
a night composed of *nows*
and thens and some-days
      and you
fellow traveller
your speech
   still shifting the dark air

Everything is moving
outside the door
listening hushed
from inside

little drifter
distant galaxies move
all rushing
why are we here
dissolve deep
breathing bodies
as waves breaking
in and out of time

Anticipating the future
as breathing
soft breath of twelve
people at dinner
or sleeping
I whisper *they are both*
you mouth
magic!
without a sound

///

if everything is moving

here is not here

not exactly here

still an elsewhere

nows

thens some-days

everything is moving

little drifter

distant galaxies move

all rushing

here

anticipating the future

as breathing

people at dinner

or sleeping

they are both

magic!

WHERE THE COSMOS OPENS OUT INTO WINTER

Approaching from the sleep side widens the acoustic field in which History is made; more bandwidth for listening in on the conversations of the twelve figures provocatively canonised in the Cosmic Oval. Who are they? Why are they there? Why are they *here*?

There is no remaining trace of a 'final' collection of names for the figures who are now depicted. Examining all the suggested names across various documents, I feel a sense of the impossibility of making a definitive selection. One document comes close: a type-written scheme for the Frieze called 'Cultural History', dated 25 July 1984.[9] Still, this has Zoser in the place of Imhotep, and 'Pericles (or Phedias?)' in the place of the figure painted by Stok as Pythagoras. I half-imagined that when I finally met Stok, he would turn through some pages of his carefully ordered plastic folders to his copy of the settled score. Such a thing, if ever it was in the world, no longer exists.

At the scale of the universe, the next part of the story – of cosmological events that took place billions of years ago – can take years, even lifetimes, to tell. Greene describes cosmic storytelling as a choreography of collective work and imagination taking place over generations, moving forward in order to move back:

> Take a moment to let this sink in. Physicists describe the earliest moments of the universe using Einstein's equations, updated to include Guth's hypothetical energy field filling space, subject to the quantum uncertainty we learned from Heisenberg. Mathematical analyses of the inflationary burst

> then reveal that it should have left an indelible imprint, a fossil of creation in the form of a specific pattern of minute temperature variations across the night sky. Sophisticated space-based thermometers built nearly fourteen billion years later by a species just coming of scientific age here in the Milky Way have now detected precisely that pattern.[10]

An indelible imprint, a fossil of creation – astrophysics in the archaeological mood makes something solid of the sky, while also bringing into human relation massive phenomena of a completely different scale. If you can imagine the imprint of a prehistoric hand on the wall of a cave, you can almost transpose the sensation of touch out there, somewhere in the universe. If you can imagine the spiralled lines of an ammonite fossil you can almost begin to discern a concrete relic preserved in the folds of deep-space.

Almost. What am I protecting with *almost*? I think the fine lines between imagination and belief.

SLEEP SONG

/

Below an *elliptical dome, suspended from the ceiling by a miracle,* twelve figures face in all directions – looking at their looking, *most speakingly the eyes. They are the only measures we have, sheer reference,* their sight lines leading not only to each other and *everything that shone* but to you: the guest, *my ghest,* a figure standing looking back asking *how the universe makes meaning of us.* To you, standing at the break in the oval where the cosmos opens out into Winter.

They live here, at the beginning of the house; in the hot blue beginnings of time. Imagine sleeping through the beginning of time, Hannah. Is that something we share? *Symbolism stops at my door, grand stranger,* you who are *not so much free* . . . as . . . *chained to the struggle for freedom?* A quiet answer stirs the distance, *how does one live with the dead.*

//

Below an *elliptical dome*
   suspended
by a miracle
twelve figures looking
most speakingly
   the eyes

only measures
have sheer reference
sight lines leading
to *everything that shone*
to you the guest
   my ghest
a figure asking
the universe where
the cosmos opens
   out into Winter

They live here
in the hot blue
beginnings of time
   imagine sleeping

Hannah

at my door

not so much

free as *chained*

for freedom

a quiet answer

how does one live

with the dead

///

elliptical dome

suspended

by a miracle

most speakingly

the eyes

only measures

sheer

everything shone

my ghest

the universe

at my door

not so much

free

for freedom

how does one live

with the dead

SIX MASTABAS OF INCREASING SIZE

In the 1960s, a mysterious static could be heard 'on an old-style television tuned to a channel that had concluded its broadcast for the evening'. Embedded in this static were traces of the Big Bang – what Brian Greene calls the 'afterglow of creation'.[11]

From *Fossil of creation* to *Afterglow of creation*; hard and soft beginnings. These atmospheric images of creation (for me, an acoustic image – something like a voiced /ɑː/ until you run out of breath) set completely different scenes for the cosmic story.[12] For the figures of the Cosmic Oval, the stories of the beginning belong to myth, religion, poetry and science. Whether the universe was created by a sleeping sun god in a primordial sea, *ex nihilo*, or by the Big Bang – there is always *the voice* in command of language, often *His*.

The uses of metaphor in science to bring things into relative terms takes us extremely close to the language of religion, sometimes purposefully. *Let there be light*, and the cosmos illuminates in *the afterglow of creation*. Language blurs the fine boundaries between imagination and belief continuously. How does one's image-belief of the world meet another's?

Against the complex star cloth of the Cosmic Oval, human time takes its temporary place in cosmic deep-time – each of the figures has a unique relationship to existence, the meaning of life, their place in the world. Jencks imagined the Frieze as 'a dialogue of individuals across time', specifically in the context of western civilisation or, as he puts it, 'the notion of a synthetic western tradition passed on from individual to individual . . . Thus Egyptian, Roman, Gothic and Modern masters speak to each other.'[13]

When we speak *with* each other, speaking is a practice of listening. I imagine the bridges that start to stretch across the Cosmic Oval – the way a particular sensibility or moral stance, a political desire or an existential melancholy start forming common threads (despite, or even because of, their diversities of thought). I have in mind so many such bridges braided with common threads that I can almost (almost) see how they arc between the twelve figures: a threaded bridge for revolution, several bridges for strange relics, many for love, all for 'reflecting deeply on mortality and eternity'.[14] Greene invites this deep reflection, gesturing to the necessity of art in telling the stories of human experience as a vital counterpoint to narratives of 'objective truth' and structures of 'scientific understanding'.[15]

As the astrophysicist storyteller Janna Levin writes, '*We* are in the questions we ask.'[16] So, who decides what counts as objective truth? We often rely on the shorthand of 'we', but who is doing the naming? Who labels what as what – and whom as whom? We (you and I) are back to the politics of naming, because to name the one-who-names is to betray the subjectivity always implicit in claims to objectivity.

The cosmologist Chanda Prescod Weinstein writes about the difficulty and potential harm of 'translating concepts laden with jargon into accessible language'.[17] She details a pervasive historical obliviousness to the naming of cosmological phenomena, especially in relation to 'dark matter' and what is at stake in the act of naming, as meaning shifts across time and context:

> The word 'dark' means different things to different people, and in fact, the phrase itself has led to widespread misunderstanding even within the community of physicists and astronomers. Few people ever stop to think that dark matter actually isn't dark. It's just invisible to light. It's transparent – more like a piece of glass than a chalkboard. I think if a Black scientist had come up with the term, 'dark matter' probably wouldn't be their phrase of choice, just like I doubt a Black scientist would have propagated the use of 'coloured' physics in particle theory.[18]

What can we do when language, which serves to divide and classify, speaks to the core of our identity – shakes something of our belonging in the world, so that our body bears the effects? How to produce an ethics of descriptive language? P.A. Skantze writes about reaching out for another's sense of the world and meeting in conversation as 'braiding a rope for a bridge towards the other side'.[19] In doing this work, she cites the philosopher Isabelle Stengers's description of those who seek out the relationship between things. They are the 'bridge-makers – weaving relations that turn a divide into a living contrast, [those] whose power is to affect, to produce thinking and feeling.'[20] But when a description on one side of a divide has become so established in language, as with 'dark matter', how can the division be made to live again in contrast?

*

I have come to see the Cosmic Oval as a place for bringing such questions: a theatre, forum, temple, parliament or court of law. The architecture is in a mutual relationship with the rituals performed within it, so that the twelve figures of the Frieze are cast and recast as audience, actors, deities, congregation, jury, plaintiffs, defendants or government. In the shape of the 'cosmic egg', the Cosmic Oval offers its own provocation for describing our place in the world; 'the challenge' of which 'is to begin without knowing'.[21]

This image of the egg as a symbol of creation is shared by many cultures[22]: a dream-image in which by turns the egg is golden; at a potter's wheel; laid by the Great Cackler; turquoise; created in primal waters; white; black; plucked from water, shaken by the stirrings of the universe. In Tibetan mythology, the cosmic egg's shell held 'the white cliff of the gods and within it, a lake'.[23] If our images of creation 'say a great deal about who we are', they also – through the example of the cosmic egg – say a great deal about the value of each one of us describing our own version of the story *to* and *with* each other, doing our own naming, revealing the subject in what might have come to appear objective; in so doing we can make even the (seemingly) simplest of single objects a diverse and complex thing.

SLEEP SONG

/

What is the name for . . . *people who shape air through buildings? I wonder if nearby stars might reveal the evidence . . . simply through the dust.* Your eyes are hard to read and I can't see your hands; we listen for incidental answers from above, about *the beauty of the house of God, the multicolour loveliness of the gems* . . . Fainter voices fall into a syncopated chorus of memory architectures: *several rooms . . . a bare room . . . a secret cave; the cave; actually two caves (no concrete evidence) . . . no windows . . . six mastabas of increasing size . . .*

In *some extraordinary site underground . . . the one who comes in peace* remains undiscovered. *Nowhere do we learn the name of his mother.*

The ellipse grows cool, voices quieten to whispers, to lullabies of spacetime and desire. *Some words are more becoming than others . . . more emphatic, more sonorous, more suited to composition.* I am thinking of composition, an art of selection and arrangement; I am still thinking of the people who house us. Of the room with no windows. Who shapes the air of the windowless room? *Her room – 14 feet, 8 inches wide and 13 feet long* – house tomb for the living. A voice sings out this *common thread: humans render each other invisible.*

//

People who shape air
if nearby stars
reveal the evidence
  simply through the dust
eyes hard to read
  your hands
we listen for answers
the beauty
 of the house
the multicolour loveliness
of the gems
fainter voices chorus

memory architectures
several rooms
  bare room secret
cave cave two caves
no evidence no
  windows
six mastabas of
increasing size

Some extraordinary site
underground
who comes in peace
undiscovered *nowhere*
learn the name
  of his mother
the ellipse grows cool
lullabies of spacetime
and desire
some words
more becoming others
more emphatic more
sonorous more suited
to composition

the room
with no windows *her*
room house tomb
humans render
each other
invisible

///

shape air

if nearby stars

reveal

dust

the beauty

house

multicolour loveliness

gems

rooms

room secret

cave cave

windows

six mastabas

increasing

extraordinary site

underground

in peace

nowhere

name

mother

words

becoming others

more emphatic more

sonorous

composition

her

room

humans

invisible

WITH A WILD MOTION, BOTH MAD AND TENDER

Jencks's papers for the Cosmic Oval show an unsettled shuffling of names in developing the idea for the gathering of figures. Reading through, I could sense a desire to include as many global perspectives as he could on cultural life and developing conceptions of the universe. I wonder if in later years he thought again about the gender landslide of the many names in the mix and the eventual twelve.[24] Among the hundreds of annotated newspaper articles Jencks kept is a review of Linda Hutcheon's 1988 *A Poetics of Postmodernism*, in which he marks the line: 'Too often scholars talk about pluralism and yet work with a totally male, white canon . . .'[25]

While the archive held at The Cosmic House presents Jencks's vision of the Cosmic Oval, it remains a fragment – like all archives it is selective, defined as much by its omissions as by what and who it reveals. Maggie Keswick Jencks's contributions are often materially obscure in the archival documents; she appears in brief as 'MK' and once in a crossed-out line noting her relationship to the Cultural History Frieze. Yet her influence runs through every scheme Jencks produced, including those bearing only his name. I've come to understand the depth of her contribution, including to the ongoing composition of the Frieze, largely through conversations – through the informal, the anecdotal.[26]

Stok finished the Frieze in the summer of 1984, when Jencks was on holiday. To find the painting completed on his return was a surprise: he had asked Stok to paint only one panel as a sample, but Stok had painted all four. When I spoke with Stok, he hinted at the respectful unsettledness of his and Jencks's working relationship, and by extension the Frieze: 'We were like two boys playing with a toy . . . we had a different point of view.' I ask if he had ever wondered at there being only one woman, among the History boys . . .

*

An in-person conversation reveals so much through facial expressions, vocal tones, the way the hands move. With what inflections and intentions does living expression find its way onto the page? Kate Briggs characterises 'reading books written by other people' as 'the everyday complicated miracle'.[27] The cast and creators of the Cosmic Oval have written many words, while others have translated them, not to mention their words preserved-as-said because another person has brought their life to the page . . . or to the airwaves of hearsay where *legend has it that . . .*

'Only through art, [Proust] noted, can we enter the secret universe of another, the only journey in which we truly "fly from star to star", a journey that cannot be navigated by "direct and conscious methods".'[28] For Marguerite Yourcenar, 'taking the habit of writing each night' for *Memoirs of Hadrian* in 1949, entering Hadrian's 'secret universe' was a devotional act achieved through deep attention: 'I could place myself intimately within another period of time.'[29] But even in a space of close, nightly communion with a distant subject, it is still a challenge to write a historical figure's voice when 'nothing, or virtually nothing, is left us of those inflections, those quarter-tones, those articulated half-smiles which yet can change everything.'[30] Writing someone into being is fraught with considerations about the illusory potential for authenticity and fidelity. Writing Hadrian's voice, Yourcenar finds eight words that refuse to be rendered in Greek or Latin: *with a wild motion, both mad and tender*. Only through the attempted process of translation does she hear the complex overlay of their voices:

> There are moments when, inadvertently, I caused him to speak the French of my day, and these eight words seem to me, as I reread them, to constitute one such moment. The reader will ask why I do not then remove them. Because the impression, if not the expression, seems authentic to me . . . after all precautions have been taken it is right to let inexactitude play its part, and even welcome the enrichments it may bring us.[31]

SLEEP SONG

/

horse-deer . . . mother-bride . . . Point at a deer and say horse. The air is now wild with words, roughly related. A railway station, a hand with no ring finger. Unfinished stories repeat with intensity. *Five Willows, the depths of your names.*

I make an acoustic leap to hear you as they would have heard you. An approach interrupted by my Classics teacher's beautiful voice moving from Latin to Ancient Greek. She called the rough spirit *a small sail,* pushing the wind into the word. I loved that image and still do. I can hear this wind, *humidity, glinting phosphors*; the breathing marks of very dark mornings when I was half asleep.

Only the mountains are missing – at this distance authenticity is of little importance . . . still, I wonder what *this distance* is, how close or simply immeasurable.

I close my eyes as two voices devote their energies to *a labour of changing words . . . little soul fleeting spirit little wild my little soul little stray wandering witching thing old ghost . . . My little wandring sportful Soule.*

//

horse deer mother
bride point at a deer
and say horse
air wild with words
roughly related
a railway station hand
with no ring finger
unfinished intensity
  five willows
depths of your
names acoustic
hear you as they would
interrupted
by my teacher's
beautiful voice
she the rough spirit

a small sail
pushing the wind
into the word
hear this wind
humidity glinting
phosphors breathing
of very dark mornings
half asleep

Only mountains
missing at this distance
authenticity of little
importance still
this distance
how close immeasurable
close my eyes
a labour of changing
words little soul
fleeting spirit little
wild my little soul
little stray wandering
witching thing
old ghost

my little
wandring
sportful
Soule

///

horse deer   mother
point at a deer
say horse

five willows
depths

a small sail

humidity glinting

phosphors

only mountains

at this distance

little

this distance

labour

words

little soul

spirit

wild *little*

little *wandering*

witching thing

little

wandring

sportful

Soule

MEN IN DARK TIMES

Hannah Arendt is the figure in the Frieze I have spent most time with.[32] The title of her 1968 book, *Men in Dark Times*, seemed to describe my initial impression of the Frieze. When I opened it, a symmetry appeared between its contents and my project. With a rush of amazement, I felt I had found an analogue: a collection of essays on ten men, although eleven 'appear' because two are about the same person. *Men in Dark Times* is, as Arendt writes in her introduction, 'primarily concerned with persons – how they lived their lives, how they moved in the world, and how they were affected by historical time'.[33]

> Even in the darkest of times we have the right to expect some illumination, and that such illumination may well come less from theories and concepts than from the uncertain, flickering, and often weak light that some men and women, in their lives and their works, will kindle under almost all circumstances and shed over the timespan that was given them on earth – this conviction is the inarticulate background against which these profiles were drawn.[34]

'They share the age in which their lifespan fell,' Arendt writes of the men (and the two women who enter the world of her book in the guise of 'men'). This is also Arendt's age – these men are her peers. The composition of Arendt's book, in turn, makes explicit that each of the twelve figures in the Cultural History Frieze is also the centre of their own cultural star map. Each historical figure has a lifetime's worth of 'navigation posts' around them. In this way, the Frieze expands; space opens up behind the twelve and there they are: a constellating cast of all those others whose lives corresponded with their own.

*

Deep in the blue, there are people whose names you and I have never heard and some maybe half-heard. Then there are some whose names, if I say them will create that glint of recognition. For example, I might say, 'her name is Sally Hemings'. Then you might say 'I know.' But what is knowing? Stay with the Frieze for long enough and the Oval becomes a peopled palace; the twelve figures conduits to 'a whole, varied, alternative history of thought'.[35]

The way these alternative histories appear to us, what they speak to us and who or what we choose to hear is significant, not least because the way we bring others into our work has real-world effects. If 'only through art . . . can we enter the secret universe of another', then the responsibility of the artist is immense. How does this responsibility change when moving from art to criticism? Maybe it is not change so much as a different kind of pressure that weighs on speculative methods, when attempting to make (to re-member) the form of the absent body – and their secret universe – in our own imagination.

The 'secret universe' we make is already structured by our ideological and philosophical architectures (with walls of varying permeabilities), which then shift to make the space for 'theirs'. To bring another's life into one's own work is always a fictionalising exercise. To read Arendt's 1957-59 essay, 'Reflections on Little Rock', is to witness what Fred Moten calls Arendt's 'brutal empathy', her 'precarious empathy'[36]; her attempt, with 'Olympian authority'[37], to imagine the thinking-feeling of another's secret universe, conditioned by her anti-Black position on desegregation in America.

Responding to 'the events at Little Rock' in 1957, a protest supported by the Arkansas National Guard against nine African-American students entering a previously segregated school, Arendt wrote an article that would remain unpublished for two years.[38] In 1959, *Dissent* published the piece with the disclaimer that 'the article was published not because the editors agreed with it but, to the contrary, because they believe in freedom of expression even for views that seem to us entirely mistaken.'[39] As Seyla Benhabib put it, the disclaimer 'anticipates the tone of shock and acrimony with which liberal white and black intellectuals were to meet [the article]'.[40] Responding to critics after publication, Arendt details her 'point of departure': a 'picture in the newspapers showing a Negro girl on her way home from a newly integrated school: she was persecuted by a mob of white children.' Arendt puts herself in the position of a 'Negro mother' by asking herself what she would do; nowhere does she name the girl.[41] This is, Benhabib writes, 'one of the rare occasions in the Arendtian corpus when she appeals to one's identity rather than to one's arguments, beliefs, and positions in public as supporting evidence for one's views.'[42]

In his extraordinary extended essay 'Refuse Refuge Refrain', Fred Moten returns the girl's name to her: 'Elizabeth Eckford in the gauntlet, on her way to school'. Moten's work aims to restore what he calls 'the collateral object' of Arendt's critique: 'to resound the depths of something serial representation threatens to reduce to one dimension':

> *Neither the 'Negro girl' nor her actions appear to Arendt.* Eckford is unseen because she is neither seen nor heard to see. More precisely, something remains unseen in Arendt's reflection(s), something given in and by Eckford's alternative vision and the revisionary passages through which she is seen. Arendt does not see what she sees and so the photograph is a speaker through which Arendt's own voice is projected. This is to say that Arendt understands Eckford to bear mute, however eloquent, witness.[43]

Through Moten's words, Elizabeth Eckford, 'in her sunglasses', is granted an agency that grows into an emblematic power of 'dark speech': a kind of speech which Moten – citing Danielle Allen – describes as 'rumor, gossip, a kind of un-authored and unauthorized speech whose origins cannot be traced'.[44]

I hear the work that one word does in dark speech, dark times and dark matter – the way particular minds make it move, and how it lands. If dark speech is, as Moten writes, something like 'the underbreath of the polis, threatening the normative order the city can be said to have agreed on', then Eckford can be heard in the Cosmic Oval: she is there too, in its underbreath. There must be many figures who make up this ensemble. 'People are trapped in history and history is trapped in them'.[45]

SLEEP SONG

/

She is standing behind you, the young girl, *eyes obscured by shadow and sunglasses. The impossibility of memory come to life.* You have all night, still you are distracted by the call of revolutions, their *lost secrets* and *violent demands; the discarded image* of an old cosmic order.

I listen to your voice echo in this expanding chorus, a song of *Men* and *dark times* and *our right to . . . illumination.* You refuse to be defined and it's a way to survive, if continuously willing to confuse what others make of you. The *right to opacity* takes work to effect, to have and maintain. This labour for one's own liberty, always also a reckoning with what needs to be protected and what needs to be said. And who does the saying? Who makes the shape of need? Our lives transform in others' hands. Your *she was not precisely happy* is another's *savage ritual.*

I get stuck here, somewhere between your brilliance and *brutal empathy*. She remains, the young girl, *in her sunglasses*. I ask if I can listen with her, from behind the Frieze; back here there is so much space – illusions of infinity, funhouse mirrors – and a tidal silence that roars with voices; the many *sent in silence to tell us there is none.*

//

She is behind you
the young girl
eyes obscured by shadow
and sunglasses
the impossibility of memory
come to life
you have all night
distracted by the call
of revolutions *lost*
secrets and *violent demands*
the discarded image
an old cosmic song
of *Men* and
dark times

our right to illumination
to survive
continuously willing
the *right to opacity*
this labour for liberty
who does the saying
who makes the shape
of need *she was*
not happy
another's *savage*
ritual she remains
the young girl
in her sunglasses
  listen
there is so much space
illusions of infinity
funhouse mirrors
and a tidal silence roars
the many
sent in silence
to tell us there is
none
///

eyes obscured by shadow

and sunglasses

the impossibility of memory

come to life

lost

secrets violent demands

discarded image

Men

dark times

illumination

opacity

she was

not happy

savage

ritual

in her sunglasses

sent in silence

to tell us there is

none

WHITE FLUORESCENT PAINT

In the Cultural History Frieze, Hannah Arendt, cigarette in hand, appears in conversation with Thomas Jefferson, a historical figure to whom she dedicates considerable attention in *On Revolution*. Jencks's copy of Arendt's 1963 book is heavily annotated, with whole passages underlined in red biro. These selections constitute a 'dialogue of individuals across time'; the writer and reader sharing an interest in the circulatory potential of speech and the preservation of human endeavours through speaking about them.

> What saves the affairs of mortal men from their inherent futility is nothing but this incessant talk about them, which in its turn remains futile unless certain concepts, certain guideposts for future remembrance, and even for sheer reference, arise out of it.[46]

If mortals are carried some way towards immortality on the frequency and volume of others' words, 'history is another name for what happens when everyone is talking all at once.'[47] The Frieze must host a cacophonous background hum, a low, steady sound carrying generations of 'incessant talk'. And so the Cosmic Oval's sonic composition both deepens and expands – to host the fragments of each figure's speech, surfacing through the drone of voices still attending to their names, and there, too, is the underbreath: before heard, felt . . .

I hear all the voices complexly, and not least Arendt's; in part because, as Moten writes, 'she remains here': a cultural figure become historical figure whose voice still moves 'on the scene that is supposed to be the American political and intellectual field'.[48] It is her *remaining here* that produces the conditions for closer scrutiny of her life and life-works and exposes the contradictions in her thinking, however serious and brilliant her thought. Every historical figure in the Frieze bears their own contradictions as they are carried through time to meet our own. Some attract a colder light, the cross-examinations of the present tense. Arendt in 1984 cuts a different figure from Arendt in the 21st century.

The image and the way it is seen change through time. The image of the universe across centuries of shifting scientific, religious and ecological ideas of the cosmos is a significant preoccupation of the Cosmic Oval. Ancient cosmologies – old models and what C.S. Lewis called 'discarded images' of the universe – collide; meaning is not fixed or absolute but plural, contingent, shaped afresh by each new observer. In *The Discarded Image*, Lewis writes: 'In every age the human mind is deeply influenced by the accepted model of the universe. But there is two-way traffic; the Model is also influenced by the prevailing temper of mind.'[49] This reciprocal relationship, between cosmological models and cultural consciousness, is at the heart of the Frieze, with each of the twelve figures engaging in their own dialogue between cultural identity and cosmic vision. Yet the Frieze, as an artwork and a conceptual model, also participates in this dynamic, shaped not only by the ideas it presents, but by the artists who brought it into being.

Charles Jencks's 'Program for the Entrance Ellipse' proposes an imaginative, composite model of the universe: what we experience through Stok's painting is a reinterpretation – a visual and material embodiment of that model. Even its physical form, its materiality, reflects the 'prevailing temper of mind' of its creators. While Stok used egg tempera, the precious medium of translucent shimmering properties, Jencks, in his only written note on the materiality of the Frieze, suggests diagrams be highlighted with the latter-day luminosity of 'white fluorescent paint'.

SLEEP SONG

/

Can we research fluorescence? You turn to me and before I can continue *(Obsessive sound – voices)* the conversation around us loudens with talk of *crystal vessels . . . twenty-five inscriptions and several shells.* How strange to hear lists of worldly things; how naming performs possession. Or dares utter the loss of the once held or inhabited; *a window on . . . a private world of wood, clay and red wax . . . 142 pictures.*

Peach and plum trees unfold in front of the hall. Closer and not closer, the oval keeps changing shape. *Matter and curvature are entwined.* Would you call this a room Gaia, the *entrance ellipse?*

The conversation quietens to listen to the spire and deep curves of St Ivo, its talismanic bees. *Something immortal achieved by mortal hands.* The architect's house, as inventoried on 3 August 1667, is revealed in the spectral words of what it contained: *hundreds of books*; paintings; many small and wonderful things.

His mother, *taken in mind*, is named for resurrection. *With deep sorrow I come back with only my walking stick.*

//

Can we research
fluorescence turn
before I can
  continue *obsessive*
sound loudens with talk
crystal vessels
inscriptions and several
shells strange
worldly possession
  the loss
once held *window*
on a private world
of *wood clay*
red wax pictures peach

and plum trees unfold
in front of the hall

Matter and curvature
entwined would you
call this a room Gaia
listen to the spire
the deep curves
of St Ivo
talismanic bees
something immortal
achieved by mortal
hands the architect's
house revealed in
spectral words
hundreds of books
  paintings
small wonderful
mother *taken in*
mind for resurrection
with deep sorrow
I come back
with only my walking stick

///

Can we research

fluorescence

obsessive

sound

crystal vessels

inscriptions and several

shells

window

on a private world

wood clay

red wax pictures   peach

and plum trees unfold

in the hall

matter and curvature

entwined

something immortal

by mortal

hands

hundreds of books

taken in

mind

with deep sorrow

come back

walking

WHO SAYS GOODBYE

Where are you coming from? You might ask this of someone composing an argument, as you might ask of an unexpected guest at your door. The question holds others within it: how did you get here? What brings you? Where are you headed? The moment of arrival, whether at a doorstep or in the articulation of an idea, is always a provisional still point. An argument or guest only ever stays in place a while – their condition is to move.[50]

To arrive at the Cosmic Oval and meet the figures of the Frieze is to experience the ways thinking-feeling travels on an epic scale through written word and hearsay, carried with the interests and investments of others.

Who we choose to bring into the ongoing composition of our own critical thought is part of the production of cultural memory. We are, each of us, involved in this work, in subtle or bold or in-between ways. Anti-colonial and feminist thinkers such as Maria Lugones, Laura Harris, P.A. Skantze and Fred Moten offer us the sensorial practice of study as social and imaginative right; study as something happening on the street[51], across 'experiments in exile'[52], in motion[53], something 'you do with other people'[54]:

> Study is what you do with other people. It's talking and walking around with other people, working, dancing, suffering, some irreducible convergence of all three, held under the name of speculative practice. The notion of a rehearsal – being in a kind of workshop, playing in a band, in a jam session, or old men sitting on a porch, or people working together in a factory – there are these various modes of activity. The point of calling it 'study' is to mark that the incessant and irreversible intellectuality of these activities was already there. These activities aren't ennobled by the fact that we now say, 'oh, if you did these things in a certain way, you could be said to be have been studying.' To do these things is to be involved in a kind of common intellectual practice. What's important is to recognize that that has been the case – because that recognition allows you to access a whole, varied, alternative history of thought.[55]

I have thought a lot about the undercommons of the Cosmic Oval. Who are those figures who occupy 'a whole, varied, alternative history of thought'? They are there too, behind or below (with you and me) the great men and the matriarch, revealing the serious absurdity and absurd seriousness of the formation of a cultural canon to represent all of human history. The impossible task of ordering such a history is akin to describing the cosmos in all its various 'images' discarded, preserved and unknown. The questions that arise from this work produce their own cultural value. These questions beat through this essay and its songs, because any resistance we put up to enclosing or re-enclosing vibrant thought into a fixed order has to wrestle with the inevitable ordering that we do, even in the course of critiquing the politics of order.

The Frieze sets everything spinning. The sincere with the ironic, the absurd with the serious, the real with the unreal. Even these opposites, like tussling balls of energy on the floor, betray my own attempts to order my thoughts.

I read Jencks's annotations on his papers in this way: as notes to buoy thought, hovering like speech. *Who says goodbye?* he writes in the margins – and I *hear* it. I love this question for what it opens up: the mystery of words not yet spoken, the anticipatory energy of an ending. *Who says goodbye?* The question accompanies the final paragraph of an early draft of the 'Program for the Entrance Ellipse':

Traditional figures might welcome the guest: the figure of Queen Nut, goddess of the sky, could be arched over the archway, welcoming in the new year. A Byzantine god might be over the front door.

By way of response, Jencks makes two handwritten additions to the end of the last line: a pair of stage directions for the Byzantine god over the entrance (also an exit) to the house. The ambivalence in the two notes casts the Entrance Ellipse as dramaturgical space, with human order a kind of stagecraft imposed on cosmic entropy. These unresolved lines – emblematic of life and ideas in continual revolution – remain as a small ode to the end as oscillation, to motion and to the lasting unsettledness of the Cosmic Oval.

A Byzantine god might be over the front door
saying "come to me"
A Byzantine god might be over the front door
to beckon goodbye.[56]

SLEEP SONG

/

Where are you going with this? a voice calls out simply and cuts through the sighs, yawns, quiet amusement and slow swaying speech. I attempt a geographical answer but you, one of you, or maybe all of you are after something different. *Life is a dream-like transformation – we lose it daily.* Where am I going with this? *Throw a pearl at hazard.*

This, your life. *This,* the collection and re-collection of small remains, the *silver shards* of luminous wisdom, cruel fables and *love-deeds,* the cosmic dreams and super-wide infinite depths. *I will tell you how it happened* . . . voices tell me how it happened and how it might . . . *make dreams truths, and fables histories.*

Enter these arms. Your extraordinary body of feelings. *Fingers in your mouths.* Bodies of lives lived, and living. So, *who says goodbye?*

Where am I going with this conversation, as *overheard from the sleep side*, arranged for a dimension both before and beyond us; a cosmic oval I might imagine we all belong to. Where am I going with my incomplete search for words to gift you space to move – with words laced, laden across centuries, words I hope carry your spirits gently enough *(sounds of wind) – sounds of water and wind.*

//

Where are you going with this?
a voice calls out simply
  cuts the sighs and
slow swaying speech
I attempt a geographical
answer something
different *life is a dream*
transformation
we lose it daily
where am I going
throw a pearl at hazard

This your life
  this collection
of small remains
silver shards luminous
wisdom cruel fables
  love-deeds
cosmic dreams
super-wide infinite depths
I will tell you how it happened
  how it might
make dreams truths
and fables histories

Enter these arms
fingers in your mouths
bodies of lives lived
and living
who says goodbye?
  overheard
from the sleep side
a dimension before beyond
imagine we belong
incomplete gift

space to move words
lace-laden across
centuries words carry
spirits gently
sounds
  sounds of
wind

///

where are you going

life is a dream

transformation

throw a pearl

this

this

silver shards

love-deeds

I will tell you

dreams

histories

enter these arms
fingers in mouths

who says goodbye

from the sleep side

sounds

sounds of
wind

CODA

A coda brings the song to an end. A beautiful sidestep from conclusion (enclosure), to pass the end of thought into sound, and into a word shared with the tail of an animal. The end as something animate – the end as alive – its movement attached to the body, while also being an agent of its own sensing of the world.

To pass the end into sound, and so back into speech, into conversation. The conversations happening, all the time, with those we choose to bring close. 'Who are my contemporaries? With whom do I live?' asks Barthes, revealing the 'optical illusion' of chronological time – those with whom we live suggest not only a spatial but a temporal arrangement.[57] Our chosen contemporaries may be untimely companions, as well as those whose lifespans fall in the same age as ours.

The conversations that do not get written exist in their remembering, reimagining, dispersal and resistance to the ordering and reduced dimensionalities of representation. History is a fantasy composed in conversation, 'in the true chaos of verbal tenses'[58], in the afterglow of creation: awake, asleep, awake, asleep, awake . . .

/a:/ until you run out of breath.

VOICES

1

if everything is moving, here is not here. Even when there is a here, it is not exactly here, but still an elsewhere

Flora Pitrolo, 'A Theatre of Many Dimensions: The Italian New Spectacularity and the Inhabitable Image', *Theatre Journal*, vol. 67, no. 4, 2015, p. 634.

nows and thens and some-days

After Emily Dickinson's 'Forever – is composed of Nows', in Thomas H. Johnson (ed.), *The Complete Poems of Emily Dickinson*, London, Little, Brown and Company, 1960, pp.307–8.

little drifter

From a translation by W.S. Merwin of Hadrian's deathbed poem included in the *Historia Augusta*. The poem, often referred to by its first line, 'Animula vagula blandula', has been translated many times across the centuries. Merwin's 2006 translation and his translator's notes can be found on the Poetry Foundation website.

distant galaxies are on the move. They're all rushing away
Brian Greene, *Until the End of Time: Mind, Matter, and Our Search for Meaning in an Evolving Universe*, London, Penguin, 2021, p. 45.

why are we here?
Author's research notes, writing in residence at The Cosmic House, July 2024.

Anticipating the future is as unavoidable and commonplace as breathing
Charles Jencks, *Architecture 2000: Predictions and Methods*, London, Studio Vista, 1971, p. 9.

people at dinner, or sleeping
Charles Jencks's annotation on a copy of his 'Program for the Entrance Ellipse', Charles Jencks Archive, CJA-TCH-a-7, Themes [1978-84].

They are both . . . magic!
Author's research notes, writing in residence at The Cosmic House, July 2024.

2

elliptical dome, suspended from the ceiling by a miracle
Charles Jencks, from 'Program for the Entrance Ellipse', Charles Jencks Archive, CJA-TCH-a-7, Themes [1978-84].

most speakingly the eyes . . .
Mary McCarthy, as cited by David Bird in 'Hannah Arendt's Funeral Held: Many Moving Tributes Paid', *New York Times*, 9 December 1975, included in Samantha Rose Hill, *Hannah Arendt*, Reaktion Books, 2021, p. 206.

they are the only measures we have
Charles Jencks, from 'Program for the Entrance Ellipse'. Charles Jencks Archive, CJA-TCH-a-7, Themes [1978-84].

sheer reference
Hannah Arendt, *On Revolution*, London, Faber & Faber, 1963, p. 222.

everything that shone

From William Stok's description of Abbot Suger, in *William Stok 1972/1993 Works and Paintings*, Treviolo, Ikonos, 1993, p. 40.

my ghest

Hadrian's 'Animula vagula blandula', translated by John Donne and included in *Ignatius His Conclave*, Oxford, Oxford University Press, 1969 [1611], p. 5.

Symbolism stops at my door

Maggie Keswick Jencks's frequently cited line, describing the threshold of her study. Edwin Heathcote and Charles Jencks, *A New Description of The Cosmic House*, London, Jencks Foundation at The Cosmic House, 2023, p. 26.

grand stranger

Mary McCarthy, 'Saying Goodbye to Hannah', *New York Review of Books*, 22 January 1976, included in Samantha Rose Hill, *Hannah Arendt*, London, Reaktion Books, 2021, p. 206.

not so much free . . . chained to the struggle for freedom

Fred Moten, *The Universal Machine*, Durham, Duke University Press, 2018, p. 87.

how does one live with the dead
Hannah Arendt, from 'Survival' [1951], a poem written to mark the death of her friend Hermann Broch, included in Samantha Rose Hill, *Hannah Arendt*, London, Reaktion Books, 2021, p. 116.

3

people who shape air through buildings
From P.A. Skantze email to the author, 27 September 2024.

I wonder if nearby stars might reveal the evidence . . . simply through the dust
Letter to Charles Jencks from D. McNally, Assistant Director of the University of London Observatory, dated 19 January 1984. Charles Jencks Archive, CJA-TCH-a-7, Themes [1978-84].

the beauty of the house of God, the multicolour loveliness of the gems
Abbot Suger, *De Administratione* (*On the Administration of the Abbey Church of Saint-Denis*) *c.*1144-48, from a translation by David Burr as part of the Internet Medieval Sourcebook, 1996.

several rooms . . . a bare room

Tao Yuanming, *Returning to Live on the Farmstead* [*c.*405 CE], translated by Michael D.K. Ing in 'Lost in Where We Are: Tao Yuanming on the Joys of Forgetting and the Worries of Being Forgotten', in Albert Galvany (ed.), *The Craft of Oblivion: Forgetting and Memory in Ancient China*, Albany, State University of New York Press, 2023, p. 335.

a secret cave; the cave; actually two caves (no concrete evidence)

Google results for the search 'did Pythagoras live in a cave?'

no windows

Description of Sally Hemings's cabin at Monticello. Jason Daley, 'Sally Hemings Gets Her Own Room at Monticello', in *Smithsonian Magazine*, July 2017.

six mastabas of increasing size

Inverted description of Imhotep's grand structure for the tomb of Djoser: 'Imhotep placed six mastabas of diminishing size on top of one another, forming the first known step pyramid.' Entry for 'Imhotep' in Michael Shalley-Jensen (ed.), *The Ancient World: Extraordinary People in Extraordinary Societies*, Ipswich, Salem Press, 2017, p. 1765.

some extraordinary site underground

Charles Jencks, a scene description in *The Seven Day Universe Outline, A Metaphysical Romance*, unpublished play-script, date unknown, p.28. Charles Jencks Archive, CJA-PTK-27.

the one who comes in peace

Charles Jencks gives this meaning to Imhotep's name in 'Maggie's Architecture: The Deep Affinities Between Architecture and Health' in *Architectural Design*, 87, 2, 2017, p.75. Sources vary over the translation of Imhotep as 'he who comes' or 'one who comes'.

Nowhere do we learn the name of his mother

John F. Benton, 'Suger's Life and Personality' in Paula Lieber Gerson (ed.), *Abbot Suger and Saint-Denis*, New York, The Metropolitan Museum of Art New York, 1986, p. 3.

some words are more becoming than others . . . more emphatic, more sonorous, more suited to composition

Desiderius Erasmus of Rotterdam, *On Copia of Words and Ideas*, translated by Donald B. King and H. David Rix, Milwaukee, Marquette University Press, 1963, p. 20.

Her room – 14 feet, 8 inches wide and 13 feet long
Jason Daley, 'Sally Hemings Gets Her Own Room at Monticello', in *Smithsonian Magazine*, July 2017. Measurements of Sally Hemings cabin at Monticello, according to the author. Exactly who made the measurements and for what purpose is unspecified, although archaeologists excavated the living quarters in 2017.

common thread: humans render each other invisible
Chanda Prescod Weinstein, *The Disordered Cosmos: A Journey into Dark Matter, Spacetime, and Dreams Deferred*, New York, Bold Type Books, 2022, p. 116.

4
horse-deer . . . mother-bride . . . Point at a deer and say horse
Various translations and etymologies of 'baka' (fool in Japanese) from Prince Ito's last words 'he is a fool', when assassinated at the Harbin Railway Station by Korean Independence activist Ahn Jung-geun on 26 October 1909. Ahn Jung-geun cut off his left ring finger with eleven other independence activists in March that year. See: Maximilian Ernst, 'On Shifting a Nation's Collective Memory: The Role of Ahn Jung-geun in South Korea's Foreign Policy',

in *Asian Journal of Peacebuilding*, 8, 2, 2020, p. 373;also, Lim Kyounghwa, 'The Role of Modern Shishi Ideals in Sympathetic Japanese Appraisals of an Chunggûn', in Acta Koreana, 20, 1, 2017, p.149; George Akita. 'Itō Hirobumi'.

Five Willows

Tao Yuanming (also known as Tao Qian and Yuanliang) wrote a short fictionalised autobiography called *The Story of the Man of Five Willows*, between *c*.42-427 CE [this version translated Fang Zhong, 2016].

depths

A translation of 渊 [yuān] that can also be read as 'deep pool'.

a small sail

Rachel Plews, the author's classics teacher from 1997 to 2000.

humidity, glinting phosphors

Matthew Fink, 'On the redomestication of feral utterance', in *after*Kleist, Pittsboro, Selva Oscura Press, 2018, p.116.

Only the mountains are missing

Maggie Keswick Jencks, *The Chinese Garden: History, Art*

and Architecture, New York, Rizzoli, 1978, p.32.

At this distance authenticity is of little importance
Marguerite Yourcenar, 'Tone and language in the historical novel', translated by Walter Kaiser, in *The New Criterion*, 8, 6, 1990, p.25.

a labour of changing words
Kate Briggs, *This Little Art*, London, Fitzcarraldo, 2017, p. 42.

little soul; fleeting spirit; little wild; my little soul; little stray; wandering witching thing; old ghost
There are many translations of Hadrian's deathbed poem, 'Animula vagula blandula':

- 'little soul': Marguerite Yourcenar, *Memoirs of Hadrian*, translated by Grace Frick, London, Penguin, 2000 [1951], p. 247.
- 'fleeting spirit': Alexander Pope, 'The Dying Christian to his Soul' in his *Selected Poetry and Prose*, edited by Robin Sowerby, London, Routledge, 1988, p. 32.
- 'my little soul': J.V. Cunningham, *Collected Poems & Epigrams*, Chicago, Swallow Press, 1971, p. 136.
- 'little stray': W.S. Merwin, 'Little Soul', in *The Shadow of Sirius*, Port Townsend, Copper Canyon Press, 2008.

Accessed on the Poetry Foundation website.

- 'little wild' and 'wandering witching thing' attributed to Charles Tennyson Turner and Dr Barclay of Edinburgh respectively, cited on Devin Coldewey's webpage collating translations from 'an 1876 volume collecting over a hundred translations of varying quality by priests, scholars, and gentlemen'. This volume remains elusive.
- 'old ghost': Nick Laird, 'To His Soul' in *Feel Free*, London, Faber & Faber, 2018, p. 72.

My little wandring sportful Soule
Hadrian's 'Animula vagula blandula', translated by John Donne, included in *Ignatius His Conclave*, p. 5.

5

eyes obscured by shadow and sunglasses
Fred Moten, *The Universal Machine*, p. 76. (Moten is referring here to Elizabeth Eckford, one of the Little Rock Nine, 1957.)

the impossibility of memory come to life
Marcia Farquhar, from a conversation with the author, 5 July 2024.

lost secrets

Charles Jencks, annotation on document titled 'Cultural History', 25 July 1984, Charles Jencks Archive, CJA-TCH-a-7, Themes [1978-84].

violent demands

Hannah Arendt, *On Revolution*, p. 245.

the discarded image

C.S. Lewis, *The Discarded Image: An Introduction to Medieval and Renaissance Literature*, Cambridge, Cambridge University Press, 1964.

Men . . . dark times

Hannah Arendt, *Men in Dark Times*, Boston, Mariner Books, 1970.

our right to . . . illumination

Hannah Arendt, *Men in Dark Times*, p. ix.

right to opacity

Édouard Glissant, *Poetics of Relation*, translated by Betsy Wing, Ann Arbor, University of Michigan Press, 1997, p. 190.

she was not precisely happy
Hannah Arendt, 'A Reply to Critics' in *Dissent*, 1959, p. 179 (after 'Reflections on Little Rock' in *Dissent*, 1959, pp. 45-56, 1959).

savage ritual
Fred Moten, *The Universal Machine*, p. 81.

brutal empathy
Ibid., p. 82.

in her sunglasses
Ibid., p. 78.

sent in silence to tell us there is none
Ibid., p. 97.

6
Can we research fluorescence?
From the author's research notes (off-cuts reformed), writing in residence at The Cosmic House, July 2024.

(Obsessive sound – voices)
William Stok, description diagram of installation *Oedipus Rex*, in *William Stok 1972/1993 Works and Paintings*, p.16.

crystal vessels . . . twenty-five inscriptions and several shells
Joseph Connors, details of Borromini's house inventory on his death (on 3 Aug 1667) in 'Francesco Borromini. La vita (1599-1667)', in R Bösel and C.L. Frommel (ed.), *Borromini e l'universo barocco*, Milan, Electa, 2000, pp.7-21, p.19.

a window on . . . a private world . . . wood, clay and red wax . . . 142 pictures
Joseph Connors, 'Francesco Borromini. La vita (1599-1667)', in *Borromini e l'universo barocco*, p. 19.

Peach and plum trees unfold in front of the hall
Tao Yuanming, Returning to Live on the Farmstead [c.405 CE], translated by Michael D.K. Ing, in Michael D.K. Ing 'Lost in Where We Are: Tao Yuanming on the Joys of Forgetting and the Worries of Being Forgotten', included in Albert Galvany (ed.), *The Craft of Oblivion: Forgetting and Memory in Ancient China*, Albany, State University of New York Press, 2023, p. 335.

Matter and curvature are entwined
Chanda Prescod Weinstein, *The Disordered Cosmos*, p. 118.

something immortal achieved by mortal hands
Hannah Arendt, *The Human Condition*, Chicago, University of Chicago Press, 2018 [1958], p. 168.

hundreds of books
Joseph Connors, 'Francesco Borromini. La vita (1599-1667)', in *Borromini e l'universo barocco*, p. 19.

taken in mind
Ibid., p. 7. Description of Borromini's mother, Anastasia.

With deep sorrow I come back with only my walking stick
Tao Yuanming, *Returning to Live on the Farmstead*, p. 336.

7
Life is a dream-like transformation
Ibid., p. 336.

even if things should last, human life does not. We lose it daily
Hannah Arendt, *Love and Saint Augustine*, Chicago, University of Chicago Press, 1996, p. 14.

Throw a pearl at hazard

Attributed to Pythagoras [c.570 to c.490 BCE] in Tyron Edwards, *A Dictionary of Thoughts: Being a Cyclopedia of Laconic Quotations from the Best Authors of the World, Both Ancient and Modern*, Detroit: F. B. Dickerson Co., 1908, p. 525. A strange artefact, the book is a collection of 'over twenty thousand thoughts' with names as their only source of reference. No known writing by Pythagoras survives.

silver shards

Flora Pitrolo, from text message, 26 August 2024.

love deeds

John Donne, 'Spring (Love's Growth)' [first published 1633], in *The Complete Poems of John Donne*, Oxford, Oxford University Press, 1990, p. 109.

I will tell you how it happened

Francesco Borromini, dictated account of his reasons for suicide, cited in Anthony Blunt, *Borromini*, Cambridge, Harvard University Press, 1979, pp. 208-9.

make dreams truths, and fables histories/Enter these arms

John Donne, 'The Dream' [first published 1633], in *The*

Complete Poems of John Donne, pp. 111-12.

Fingers in your mouths
William Stok, describing his depiction of Hadrian and Abbot Suger, in an email to the author on 21 September 2024.

who says goodbye?
Charles Jencks, annotation on 'Program for the Entrance Ellipse'. Charles Jencks Archive, CJA-TCH-a-7, Themes [1978-84].

overheard from the sleep side
From author's research notes (responding to Anne Carson), writing in residence at The Cosmic House, July 2024.

(sounds of wind)
William Stok, detail from diagrammatic score for installation 'Past, Present, Future', in *William Stok 1972/1993 Works and Paintings*, p. 18.

sounds of water and wind
Maggie Keswick Jencks, *The Chinese Garden: History, Art and Architecture*, p. 106.

ENDNOTES

1 Charles Jencks, *Towards a Symbolic Architecture*, New York, Rizzoli, 1985, p. 109.
2 Anne Carson, *Decreation*, New York, Knopf, 2005, p. 20.
3 Ibid.
4 Ibid.
5 Aristotle, in Jonathan Barnes (ed.), *The Complete Works of Aristotle Vol. 2*, translated by A. Platt, Princeton, Princeton University Press, 1984, p. 1204.
6 There are four identical copies of the 'Program for the Entrance Ellipse', with varying degrees of annotation, in the Charles Jencks Archive, alongside two versions of the program I think of as a 'Proto-program', the work in development. CJA-TCH-a-7, Themes [1978-84].
7 Charles Jencks, 'Program for the Entrance Ellipse' in Charles Jencks Archive, CJA-TCH-a-7, Themes [1978-84].
8 Brian Greene, *Until the End of Time: Mind, Matter, and Our Search for Meaning in an Evolving Universe*, London, Penguin, 2021, p. 5.
9 Charles Jencks, 'typescript notes titled "Cultural History July 25th 1984 MK CK WS" relating to the frieze' in Charles Jencks Archive, CJA-TCH-a-7, Themes [1978-84].

10 Greene, *Until the End of Time*, p. 51.
11 Ibid., p. 48.
12 Incidentally I realise, the ɑː sound in my voice is in Father and Amen and also in Afterglow.
13 Jencks, 'Program for the Entrance Ellipse', Charles Jencks Archive, CJA-TCH-a-7, Themes [1978-84].
14 Greene, *Until the End of Time*, p. 240.
15 Ibid., p. 235.
16 Janna Levin, 'The truth of lies', *New Scientist*, 191:2565, 2006 pp. 44-5. Italics added. Here, Levin also talks about the 'social agreement' in technical articles to use the royal 'we'.
17 Chanda Prescod Weinstein, *The Disordered Cosmos: A Journey into Dark Matter, Spacetime, and Dreams Deferred*, New York, Bold Type Books, 2022, p. 122.
18 Ibid., p. 125.
19 P.A. Skanzte, 'Take me to the Bridge', in Mariella Greil, Emma Cocker and Nikolaus Gansterer (ed.), *Choreo-Graphic Figures*, Berlin, De Gruyter, 2017, p. 176.
20 Isabelle Stengers [2012] in Skantze, 'Take me to the Bridge', in *Choreo-Graphic Figures*, p. 176.
21 Skantze, 'Take me to the Bridge', in *Choreo-Graphic Figures*, p. 179.
22 David Leeming, 'Cosmic Egg', in *The Oxford Companion to World Mythology*, Oxford, Oxford University Press, 2005, p. 82. 'In many creation myths – including some in China, Japan, Egypt, Borneo, Finland, Greece, and Tibet, and especially India, as, for instance, in the myth of Brahma, the pre-creation void takes the form of an egg, sometimes a golden one.'
23 Ibid., p. 383.
24 See the Jencks Foundation at The Cosmic House website for a composite list made by the author of every historical figure (and themes/countries) mentioned in Charles Jencks's working papers towards the Cultural History Frieze.

25 Wendy Steiner, 'A game or a squabble?', publication unknown. Found in *A Poetics of Postmodernism: History, Theory, Fiction* (London, 1988) by Linda Hutcheon, in Charles Jencks's library at The Cosmic House [uncatalogued].
26 A notebook Keswick Jencks kept between 1982 and 1983 offers further insight into her meticulous attention to the House. Its rediscovery, by artist Marysia Lewandowska, seemingly by chance – in the night – reveals a sustained authorship in her working on the House's design.
27 Kate Briggs, *This Little Art*, London, Fitzcarraldo Editions, 2017, p. 171.
28 Greene, *Until the End of Time*, p. 237, quoting Marcel Proust, *Remembrance of Things Past*, vol. 3, translated by C.K. Scott Moncrieff, New York, Vintage, 1982, p. 260 and p. 931.
29 Marguerite Yourcenar, *Memoirs of Hadrian*, translated by Grace Frick, Penguin, 2000 [1951], p. 283.
30 Marguerite Yourcenar, 'Tone and language in the historical novel', translated by Walter Kaiser, in *The New Criterion*, 8, 6, 1990, p. 26.
31 Ibid., p. 28.
32 'I began to track her among the elegant tissue of echoes, quotations, shadows . . .' Lisa Robertson, *XEclogue*, Vancouver, New Star Books, 1999, unpaginated.
33 Hannah Arendt, *Men in Dark Times*, New York, Harcourt, Brace & World, 1968, p. vii.
34 Ibid., p. ix. Arendt borrows 'dark times' from Bertolt Brecht's poem 'To Posterity', written in exile between 1934 and 1938.
35 S. Harney and F. Moten, *The Undercommons: Fugitive Planning and Black Study*, New York, Minor Compositions, 2013, p. 110.
36 Fred Moten, *The Universal Machine*, Durham, Duke University Press, 2018, p. 82.
37 Ralph Ellison, cited in Seyla Benhabib, *The Reluctant Modernism of Arendt*, Thousand Oaks, California, Sage, 1996, p. 154.

38 Hannah Arendt, 'Reflections on Little Rock' in *Dissent*, 6:1,1959, p. 46.
39 Editors of *Dissent*, cited in Benhabib, *The Reluctant Modernism of Arendt*, p. 146.
40 Ibid.
41 Hannah Arendt,'A Reply to Critics' in *Dissent*, 6:2, 1959, p. 179.
42 Benhabib, *The Reluctant Modernism of Arendt*, p. 148.
43 Moten, *The Universal Machine*, p. 75.
44 'Allen writes of the distinction between dark speech (rumor, gossip, a kind of un-authored and unauthorized speech whose origins cannot be traced, thereby placing it in a kind of illegitimate adjacency to divine power) and speech whose origins are visible, in the light of day, emerging from a place in the sun in which the rights and obligations of publicness, and the power to be seen, can be assumed ... The relative silence of a certain darkness of speech constitutes something like the underbreath of the polis, threatening the normative order the city can be said to have agreed upon.'
45 James Baldwin,'Stranger in the Village', in Toni Morrison (ed.), *James Baldwin: Collected Essays*, New York, Library of America, 1998, p. 119.
46 Hannah Arendt, *On Revolution*, London, Faber & Faber, 1963, p. 222.
47 Jordan Alexander Stein, *Fantasies of Nina Simone*, Durham, Duke University Press, 2024, p. 2.
48 Moten, *The Universal Machine*, p. 74.
49 C.S. Lewis, *The Discarded Image: An Introduction to Medieval and Renaissance Literature*, Cambridge, Cambridge University Press, 1964, p. 222.
50 In his unpublished manuscript 'Meaning in the Cosmos', Charles Jencks writes similar questions: 'Identity is formed through recounting many stories which explain our position and orientation to others ... We say "where is he coming from? Where are you

going?" Such orientation-questions help define a destiny and a series of them end up defining an autobiography.' Charles Jencks Archive, uncatalogued, p. 13.

51 Maria Lugones, 'Tactical Strategies of the Streetwalker'/ 'Estrategias Tácticas de la Callejera' in *Pilgrimages/Peregrinajes: Theorizing Coalition Against Multiple Oppressions*, Oxford, Rowman & Littlefield, 2003, pp. 222-40.

52 Laura Harris, *Experiments in Exile: C.L.R. James, Hélio Oiticica, and the Aesthetic Sociality of Blackness*, New York, Fordham University Press, 2018.

53 P.A. Skantze, *Stillness in Motion in the Seventeenth-Century Theatre*, New York, Routledge, 2003.

54 S. Harney and F. Moten, *The Undercommons*, p. 110.

55 Ibid.

56 From two separate copies of the 'proto-programs' for the Entrance Ellipse, Charles Jencks Archive, CJA-TCH-a-7, Themes [1978-84].

57 Roland Barthes, *How to Live Together*, translated by Kate Briggs, New York, Columbia University Press, 2012, pp. 5-6. See also Briggs, *This Little Art*, p. 17.

58 Hélène Cixous, *Stigmata*, translated by Eric Prenowitz, Oxford, Routledge, 2005 [1998], p. 190.

AFTERWORD

What is history and how is it made? What does it mean, within the frame of artistic practice, to open up archives? With Ella Finer, The Cosmic House co-hosted a series of salons exploring these questions: an inherently polyphonic and collective exercise that, at the same time, was highly subjective and necessarily autobiographical. Later, from summer 2024 until late spring 2025, Finer was a resident at The Cosmic House, a newly opened museum that houses the personal archive of a postmodern historian and writer, where the matter of writing history remains a central enquiry.

The Cosmic House is an archive of ideas, an eclectic collage of quotations and historic references, and a means of postmodern world-building for its former inhabitants, the architectural critic and historian Charles Jencks and his wife, the artist and garden designer Maggie Keswick Jencks. In his search for meaning in architecture, or an 'architecture that speaks', Jencks suggested that the fundamental elements of building – doors, windows, columns, and so on – could be understood as a linguistic system. Originally a Victorian townhouse, The Cosmic House (initially named 'The Symbolic House' or 'The Thematic House') was extensively redesigned and transformed between 1978 and 1983. Its complex symbolic programme presents seventeen themes weaving together historic styles and references, irony, and a deep engagement with science and cosmology. This cosmic ensemble of rooms and interiors is co-created with numerous friends and collaborators who Charles and Maggie invited to the project, ranging from figures such as Michael Graves and Terry Farrell to Eduardo Paolozzi. Today, this unique architectural Gesamtkunstwerk in London's Holland Park, considered among the most important examples of postmodern domestic architecture, is open to visitors as a Grade I listed museum. It is also a convivial site for residencies and new artistic and scholarly commissions that create meaning through engaging, expanding, or debating ideas imbued in its interiors.

Finer was invited to respond to the Cultural History Frieze, a work which spans the entrance hall (known as 'the Cosmic Oval') of The Cosmic House. With its planetary motifs as well as references to the myth of the 'cosmic egg', this significant architectural feature within The Cosmic House embodies Charles's vision of postmodern cosmology: a worldview that unites science, religion and ecology in a new understanding of our place and meaning in the cosmos. At the heart of the Cosmic Oval is William Stok's Cultural History Frieze, commissioned by Charles and Maggie. The Frieze portrays a diverse assembly of influential figures arranged as in the iconography of the Last Supper, from the ancient Egyptian architect Imhotep to Hannah Arendt, through Pythagoras, Hadrian and Erasmus, among others. Each character appears with an attribute that reveals their main contribution to science and architecture; each represents a distinct era, region and intellectual tradition. In their assembly, as they congregate for a cosmic supper, they symbolise humanity's quest for understanding in architecture, science, philosophy and the arts.

The Frieze is a diagram of time that confronts ideas and ideologies through flattening temporal hierarchies, portraying the intellectual history of humankind as a fleeting and quasi-domestic moment in the broader context of the cosmic story. Finer's seven Sleep Songs – echoing the seven concentric layers of the Cosmic Oval in the vestibule of The Cosmic House – are distinct but overlapping takes on the Cultural History Frieze, testament to Finer's forensic research into the Charles Jencks Archive as well as a conscious reflection on her own contemporary and highly personal reading. Finer's thoughtfully constructed essay is a complex mesh of interwoven quotations, both an attitude and a method, which mirrors the pluralism of the Cultural History Frieze and exposes the temporal and ideological relativity that any singular narrative might present – including Charles's own.

The Cultural History Frieze is an intellectually omnivorous and hugely ambitious attempt. Like Charles's *Evolutionary Trees of Architecture*, ever-evolving diagrams that helped to map his theories and speculations about immediate futures as they unfolded, the Frieze is also a map – it charts 2,000 years of human history through a lineage of twelve thinkers. The inevitable omissions are almost as telling as the inclusions, and the painting eventually reveals more about its present time than any other. As Finer points out, however formalised and final the mural might appear, it captures an arbitrary moment, a snapshot of ideas in evolution which Charles kept revising throughout his lifetime. While the Cultural History Frieze does not exist in any other version, its core ideas and propositions are carried through the framework of the decade-long series of 'Portrack seminars' hosted by Charles, Maggie and a close-knit group of scholars in the 1990s. These provided the basis for Charles's later work and found expression through his land art – such as The Garden of Cosmic Speculation in Portrack or the Crawick Multiverse – and his unpublished manuscript 'Meaning in Cosmos'.

Finer's *The Cosmic Oval* is a critical, lyrical response that delicately animates William Stok's mural. Delving into Charles's universe, she reconstructs the figures on the Jencksian Oval as 'strange attractors' that sustain a multitude of ideas, personae and voices. Charles observed that the history of science reveals a parallel and intrinsically interconnected history of culture. Each scientific paradigm is conditioned by its own distinct cultural bias and is part of an epistemological cycle, calling for a continuous mode of rewriting and evolving history. In return, Finer's carefully orchestrated writing – as it moves between prose and poetry – suggests a Cosmic Oval of her own, drawn in and around the constellations of her personal cosmos. It points to the way we all invent and narrate our private intellectual and personal cosmologies and opens new entries to Charles's fundamental questions about our collective: what are we, where do we come from?

Eszter Steierhoffer
Director, Jencks Foundation at The Cosmic House

EDITOR'S NOTE

This essay 'enters from the sleep side' – each section is followed by a 'sleep song' – and hushes a busy space, turning its buzz into a hum. This is a nocturnal essay because of the kind of analysis it creates the conditions for, and one where the object of analysis can be grasped even in its continuous motion. It frees writing from the anxiety of enclosure: there is no ring around this essay. It accepts that just as a map is not the territory, a calendar is not time. In this *ringlessness*, this partiality in the key of forever (or never), I like to think Finer provides Jencks's project for the Cosmic Oval with something like a liberation. I can imagine him annotating his lists of luminaries; I can hear Finer's /ɑː/ until she runs out of breath in the Coda. The animal tail slips out of one of the seventeen doors.

Finer and Jencks seem to me to be separated not so much by time, but by the way they treat time – which is not so much to do with the epochs they are writing in and from (so near, so far) but with their conceptions of how time works. Jencks thrived in the complexity of the postmodern jump and influenced its formation. An architect working after the spatial turn in critical thought, yet so profoundly historical in his thinking, Jencks seemed to historicise the present as it happened – to intercept and name the beginnings of things. Finer seems to me to meet this historical moment, and this monument, in a state of 'postmodern swoon' (a term borrowed from theatre scholar Elinor Fuchs' description of spectatorship). As a writer and as a woman in today's shade of dark times, she finds ways to mistrust monuments and yet respect them enough to turn the dial to listen; hear the unheard in the static of the television set; flatten time so that it all folds into a single dimensionality and then stretch it out again into galaxies where she can no longer see where it goes. Writing from a time less and less interested in historicising, Finer reveals the difficulty of singling out the luminaries of the Cultural History Frieze in the context of a cogent invisibility, of dark matter. She writes, 'Stay with the Frieze for long enough and the Oval becomes a peopled palace.' She is saying that the encounter with the historicising efforts of others requires a long time – that a project like the Cosmic Oval needs to be afforded some kind of long linearity, before the edit, before awe and before polemics.

Finer recurrently draws our attention to two qualities of movement in the Cosmic Oval: the pull towards the systemic, complete and canonical on the one hand, and the hovering unsettledness, incompleteness and impossibility of the entire endeavour on the other. This tension can be productively mapped onto the strange scrapyard to which much postmodern thinking has been relegated: bizarrely grand in its prophesying and precipitated so vertiginously by the way things unfolded that it never really grew from paradigm into a praxis. Words like *periphery*, *fragmentation*, *incredulity* now strike us as naive, and essentially modernist after all. In this sense, Finer's mode of inquiry into the Oval and its swooning provisionality – this nocturnal alertness that listens in the dark – can be viewed as a proposal for a new historiographical method for postmodernity dedicated not only to understanding it as an exhibit from the museum but to intercepting its usefulness for the present. The Sleep Songs, lyrical assemblages of voices falling through time, through the sky of Finer's acoustic imagination, are the lynchpin of her method *because* they are called songs. I invite the reader to sing them as she reads, to hum them to herself to find a music, where the starry fabric of this essay hardens, an acoustic net over the Frieze as we gaze up, and up, until we can no longer see where time goes.

Flora Pitrolo

ACKNOWLEDGEMENTS

I'm grateful to the Jencks Foundation at The Cosmic House, particularly to Eszter Steierhoffer, who offered me valuable time to think, talk and listen, and to Lily Jencks for her continuous generosity. Thanks to Gaia Giacomelli and Anna McNally for their thoughtful guidance, and to Martyna Jurkevičiūtė, Flo Main, Emma Virdi, Jessica Lawson and Lev Bratishenko for their support. My extended thanks to Marysia Lewandowska for first inviting me to The Cosmic House and to Lina Lapelytė, Nouria Bah, Anat Ben-David, Angharad Davies, Sharon Gal and Rebecca Horrox for setting several of the Sleep Songs to music.

This writing has been composed alongside many conversations and I'm especially appreciative of the voices I hear in and between the lines: Canan Batur, Olive Finer

Butler, Denna Cartamkhoob, Sheila Chukwulozie, Edie Culshaw, Kate Donovan, Jeanie Farquhar, Jem Finer, Jessica Finer, Kitty Finer, Matthew Fink, Imogen Free, Emma McCormick Goodhart, Joe Hales, Max Hales, Sammy Hales, Khadra Ibrahim, Robert Jack, Helen Kaplinsky, Iris Long, Vibeke Mascini, Arjuna Neuman, Yewande Odunubi, Louise O'Hare, Iris Francesca Jack Pitrolo, Sophie Seita and Andrea Zarza. Special thanks to P.A. Skantze for reading drafts with vibrant attention and to William Stok for sharing his memories with me. My heartfelt gratitude to Marcia Farquhar for accompanying me always through her reading, responding, expanding, as well as for the enduring – cosmic – influence of her storytelling.

My great appreciation to Silver Press for giving this essay the form of a book. And finally, my deepest thanks to Kate Briggs, Flora Pitrolo and Sarah Shin for their insight, imagination and editorial precision. Each has shaped what this essay has become.

Ella Finer's work spans writing, composing and curating, with a particular focus on the ways bodies acoustically disrupt, challenge and change relations of power. Her research frequently queries the ownership of cultural expression, often through collaborative projects that centre listening as a practice of deep attention and reciprocity, as in *Silent Whale Letters*, published by Sternberg Press in 2023. Her forthcoming work, *Acoustic Commons and the Wild Life of Sound*, is a series of essays exploring how sound resists categorisation in the archive.